Jewish Holidays in the Spring

Dianne M. MacMillan

Reading Consultant:

Michael P. French, Ph.D.
Bowling Green State University

—Best Holiday Books—

ENSLOW PUBLISHERS, INC.

Bloy St. & Ramsey Ave.	P.O. Box 38
Box 777	Aldershot
Hillside, N.J. 07205	Hants GU12 6BP
U.S.A.	U.K.

Acknowledgments

The author wishes to thank Rabbi Israel Gordon of the Rabbinical College of America, Morristown, N. J., for his careful review of the manuscript; Dr. Ruth Raphaeli, coordinator of the Hebrew Language Program at Columbia University, for her review of the Hebrew language and pronunciations used in the text; Rabbi Shelton J. Donnell of Temple Beth Sholom of Orange County, Ca.; and Susanne Kester, Media Resources Coordinator, Skirball Museum, Hebrew Union College, Los Angeles.

Library of Congress Cataloging-in-Publication Data

MacMillan, Dianne.
  Jewish holidays in the spring / Dianne M. MacMillan.
      p. cm. — (Best holiday books)
  Includes index.
  ISBN 0-89490-503-1
  1. Fasts and feasts—Judaism—Juvenile literature. I. Title. II. Series.
  BM690.M23 1994
  296.4'3—dc20   93-46188
                                                   CIP
                                                     AC

Printed in the United States of America

10 9 8 7 6 5 4 3 2 1

Illustration Credits: Clay Miller/The Orange County Register, p. 39; Dianne M. MacMillan, pp. 34, 42; From the collection of Hebrew Union College, Skirball Museum, Los Angeles, pp. 4, 6, 8, 13, 15, 16, 19, 22, 26, 29, 30; Marilyn Gould, pp. 24, 25, 32.

Cover Illustration: Charlott Nathan

Contents

A Holiday Filled With Laughter 5

The Jewish Religion 9

Purim 11

How Passover Began 17

Getting Ready for Passover 21

Seder 23

Yom Ha-Atsma'ut 35

Lag B'Omer 37

Shavuot 41

Glossary 44

Index 47

Purim is a holiday filled with laughter. This painting shows an 1893 Purim celebration in a synagogue.

A Holiday Filled With Laughter

Children parade around the room. Everyone is wearing a costume. Many girls dress like queens. Some of the boys dress like kings. Others wear masks and black robes. There are noisemakers, and some people play music. Boys and girls clap and cheer. All of this noise brings laughter. This is part of Purim (poo-RIM), a Jewish holiday.

The long winter is almost over. Spring is near. It is time for five holidays that Jewish people love to celebrate. These are Purim, Passover or Pesach (PE-saḥ), Lag B'Omer (LAG ba-O-mer), Yom Ha-Atsma'ut (YOM ha-ats-ma-OOT), and Shavuot (sha-voo-OT).

Like most Jewish holidays, each one celebrates something special that happened in Jewish history.

Purim is about a brave Jewish queen named Esther. She lived long ago in Persia. Because of her bravery, the Jewish people were saved from death.

Passover, or Pesach, lasts for seven or eight days. It is a celebration of freedom. Jews recall the time when their ancestors were slaves in Egypt. God sent Moses to lead the Jewish

This pencil and watercolor drawing shows a family celebrating Passover in 1930.

people to freedom. Passover is celebrated by Jews all over the world. There are special foods, prayers, songs, and customs.

Yom Ha-Atsma'ut is the newest holiday. It celebrates the day when the country of Israel was founded in 1948. Two weeks later Lag B'Omer is celebrated. This day remembers the brave deeds of two rabbis.

The last holiday, Shavuot, takes place seven weeks after Passover. This day celebrates the spring harvest. It also celebrates the time when God gave the Ten Commandments to Moses. All five holidays bring Jewish families together. It is a time of sharing, remembering, and thanking God.

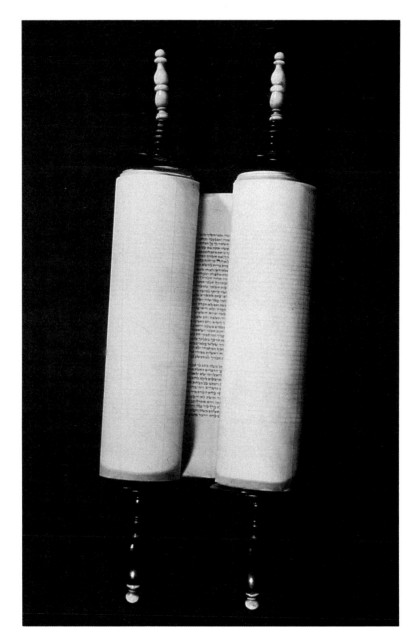

The Torah contains the first five books of the Bible.

The Jewish Religion

The Jewish religion is thousands of years old. It is called Judaism. Hebrew is the language of Judaism. It is also the language of the Jewish people. Jewish people pray in a building called a synagogue. Each week the Sabbath begins on Friday before sunset. It ends after sundown on Saturday. The Sabbath is the holiest day of the week. It is a day of rest. It is also a day to pray and enjoy family meals.

The early history of the Jewish people is written in the Torah (to-RAH). The Torah contains the first five books of the Bible. The Torah is very important to Jews.

The months in the Jewish calendar are based on the moon. A new month begins on a new moon. Holidays begin before sunset and last until after sunset on the following day. Most Jewish holidays remember things that happened thousands of years ago.

Purim

Purim is a joyous holiday. Halloween and Mardi Gras are like Purim. Purim occurs on the fourteenth day of the Jewish month of Adar (a-DAR). This is sometime in late February or early March. Twenty-five-hundred years ago a king in Persia wanted a wife. He held a beauty contest to find a queen. A young girl named Esther was chosen. The king did not know that Esther was Jewish.

One day Esther's cousin Mordecai heard two soldiers talking. They were planning to kill the king. Mordecai told the guards. The evil men were caught. The king was safe.

The king's chief advisor was Haman. Haman wanted everyone in the kingdom to bow down to him. Mordecai refused. Jews bow only to God. Haman was furious with Mordecai. He wanted to kill all the Jews living in Persia.

Haman told the king lies about the Jewish people. The king believed the lies. He told Haman he could kill the Jews. Haman threw small stones on the ground to decide the best time to carry out his plan. These stones were called lots. They looked like dice. The lots landed on thirteen and twelve. Haman believed this to mean the thirteenth day of the twelfth month. The twelfth month on the Jewish calendar is Adar. The Persian word for lots is "purim." This is where the holiday's name comes from.

Mordecai went to Queen Esther. He told her she was the only one who could save her people. She was frightened but agreed to help. She told Mordecai to ask the Jewish people to fast and pray for three days. (Fasting means to eat no food.) At the end of the three days, she would speak to the king.

When the time came Esther told the king that she was Jewish. If Haman killed all the Jews, then she must die too. She told the king about Haman's lies. He remembered how Mordecai had saved his life. The king was grateful to Queen Esther.

The king became angry at Haman. He ordered Haman to be hanged. Then the king

This silver case holds a scroll that tells Esther's story. The case is from the 19th century.

made Mordecai his new advisor. The fourteenth day of Adar became a day of celebration.

Some Jewish people fast the day before Purim. This is called Esther's fast. On the eve of Purim, everyone gathers at the synagogue. Children dress up in costumes. Many people wear masks. There is a Purim parade. Some synagogues have a Purim carnival. There are games and rides. A favorite game is to throw darts at a cardboard picture of Haman.

In some synagogues, the story of Esther is read from a scroll called the Megillah (me-gi-LAH). Every time Haman's name is read, everyone boos. Children twirl noisemakers called groggers. People stamp their feet, boo, and hiss. When Esther's name is read, they cheer.

Sometimes children act out the story. Then everyone eats. There are always special treats. Some Jews eat cakes or cookies called hamantaschen (HA-man-TA-shen). They are filled with a mixture of chopped prunes or poppy seeds and honey. The cakes have three corners and are shaped like triangles.

Some say that the cakes are three-cornered because Haman wore a three-cornered hat. Others say the cakes are shaped like Haman's pocket or ear. Whatever the reason, they are delicious. Children cannot wait to eat them.

This is a metal Purim grogger used in the United States.

MOSES.

Moses was sent by God to the pharoah. He begged the
pharoah to let the Jewish people leave Egypt.

How Passover Began

Passover celebrates freedom from slavery. In Hebrew the word for this holiday is Pesach. It is the most widely celebrated of all Jewish holidays. Jews have observed this holiday for over three thousand years. It begins on the fifteenth day of the Jewish month of Nisan (ni-SAN). This is sometime in March or April.

Long ago the Jewish people were slaves in Egypt. They built tombs and pyramids for the king who was called the pharaoh.

God sent Moses and his brother Aaron to the pharaoh. They begged the pharaoh to let the Jewish people leave. But the pharaoh did not want to lose his slaves. God punished the pharaoh by sending plagues. (A plague is something that causes disease or great misfortune.)

The crops were ruined. The cattle died. People became sick. Darkness covered the land. Still the pharaoh would not let the slaves have their freedom.

Finally God sent the last plague. This was the worst one of all. The firstborn child in each Egyptian family would be killed.

The Jewish people were told to prepare a lamb for dinner. Blood from the lamb was to be smeared above their doors. This would be a sign that this was a Jewish house. That night the plague would "pass over" the houses of the Jewish people. This is why the holiday is called Passover.

When the firstborn died, the pharaoh agreed to let the slaves leave. They packed quickly. With all their animals and belongings, the people followed Moses into the desert.

After a few days, the pharaoh changed his mind. He wanted the slaves back. He ordered his soldiers to capture them. The Jews got as far as the Red Sea. They were trapped. Then Moses held up his hands, and a miracle took place. The waters of the sea parted. There was a dry path for the Jews to walk on. They crossed quickly to the other side.

When the Egyptian soldiers followed, the waters of the sea closed in on them. The soldiers

This painting shows the drowning of the Egyptians in the Red Sea.

drowned. The Jewish people were free. This story is called Exodus. It is written in the Bible. It is one of the most important events in Jewish history.

Every year for one week, Jews remember how God saved them. They tell the story of how they were "passed over" by the death plague. Their children learn how their ancestors were freed from Egypt and about the miracles of God.

Getting Ready for Passover

A month before Passover people start getting ready. Houses are swept clean. Everything must shine and look new. Families put out dishes, silverware, and pots and pans that are used only during Passover. Often people buy new clothes. Everything is done to show that this is a special time.

Most important of all, breads, cookies, pasta, and crackers are used up. There can be no leavened bread in the house during Passover. (Leavening is anything like yeast or baking powder that allows bread to rise before baking.)

The bread and other food are replaced during Passover by matzah (ma-TSAH). Matzah is a special type of cracker made from dough that has not risen. It reminds the Jewish people of the Exodus. When their ancestors followed Moses out of Egypt, they were in a hurry and did not have time to let their bread dough rise. Matzah and matzah meal are used during Passover to make delicious cakes, cookies, pancakes, and matzah balls for soup.

This painting from 1904 shows a matzah factory.

Seder

On the first two nights of Passover, there is a special dinner. It is called a Seder (SE-der). Seder means "order" in Hebrew. This meal has a special order for everything that happens. The Seder has become the main part of the Passover celebration. During this meal, there are prayers, songs, and readings from the Bible. Everyone is reminded about the meaning of the holiday.

There are fourteen parts to the seder meal. Not all families follow the exact order from start to finish. Each family decides how they will celebrate. But most Seders take several hours to complete.

Family and friends join together. An old Jewish saying says that no one should be alone on Passover. The table is set with the family's best candlesticks, tablecloths, china, and silver. The head of the family is the leader for the Seder meal.

At each place are wine glasses and small bowls of salt water. In front of the leader's chair, there is a special plate. It is called the Seder plate. On the plate are five different foods. Each food has a special meaning. The foods are a hard-boiled egg, a roasted lamb bone, greens

Friends and family join together for the Seder meal.

(usually parsley), bitter herbs (usually small white roots of horseradish), and a mixture of fruit, nuts, and wine. This mixture is called haroset (ḥa-RO-set).

There are also three pieces of matzah covered with a cloth. The cloth has beautiful designs on it. Sometimes there is a special matzah holder made from silver or ceramic. It has a place for the Seder plate on top.

The hard-boiled egg has several meanings. It

The Seder plate holds a hard-boiled egg, a roasted lamb bone, greens, bitter herbs, and haroset.

stands for life and rebirth. It also reminds people of the offerings brought to the Jewish temple long ago. The lamb bone reminds them of the lamb's blood that was put over the door. The greens are symbols of springtime. The haroset reminds them of the mortar used by the slaves. (Mortar was the mixture that held the bricks together.) The bitter herbs remind them of the bitterness of slavery. Salt water stands for

Many times the matzah on a Seder table is covered with a beautiful cloth. This is a velvet and silk embroidered cover from Jerusalem.

tears that were shed. It also stands for the salt water of the Red Sea that the Jews crossed. The matzah reminds them of the night they left Egypt.

The leader sits on a pillow. He or she sits in a relaxed or reclining position. This was how free men and women dined long ago. In some homes, everyone sits on a pillow.

Four cups of wine will be drunk during the meal. The children will have grape juice. An extra cup of wine is filled and placed on the table for Elijah. Elijah was a famous prophet in the Bible. (A prophet is a person who gives messages from God.) Elijah is the invisible guest.

Like every Sabbath or holiday dinner, the meal begins with the lighting of the candles. A blessing is said. Then the leader says a blessing over the wine. Using a pitcher filled with water, a bowl, and cloth, he or she washes his or her hands. Sometimes the water and cloth are passed around for everyone at the table.

Now the leader dips the greens in the salt water. The greens are passed around for everyone to taste. Some families have a Seder plate for each person.

The leader uncovers the three pieces of matzah. The middle piece of matzah is broken in half with a loud crack. The larger half is hidden when no one is looking. This piece of matzah is called the afikoman (a-fi-ko-MAN). Afikoman is a Greek word that means "dessert".

Later on the children will search the house and try to find the afikoman. Whoever finds it gets a prize. Sometimes all the children get a prize. In some families, the children hide the afikoman. Then the leader has to give a gift to get it back. Often the afikoman is put in a special pouch.

It is time for the youngest child at the table to ask questions. First the child asks, "Why is this night different from all other nights?" Then he or she asks four more questions, "Why on this night do we eat unleavened bread? Why do we eat bitter herbs? Why do we dip in the salt water? Why do we sit in a relaxed position?"

The leader reads from a book called the Haggadah (ha-ga-DAH). Haggadah means "telling" or "story" in Hebrew. It explains what the Seder food means and answers the four questions. The Haggadah also has songs and blessings in it. Sometimes the Haggadah is a small booklet with pages stapled together. Often it is a beautifully illustrated book. In many

This is a German Haggadah for children.

families, each person has their own copy of the Haggadah.

The Haggadah tells how the Jews first went to Egypt. Then the story recalls how the Jews became slaves. It goes on with the birth of Moses and how he helped his people.

As the leader reads about the plagues that God sent, everyone dips their little finger in their wine. A drop of wine is spilled onto their

Sometimes the afikoman is hidden in a special pouch. This satin embroidered pouch is from the 19th century.

plate for each plague. Everyone repeats the name of the plague. This is called "the Lessening of Our Joy." Egyptians were also children of God. Jews are sorry that the Egyptians had to suffer.

Now everyone sings "Dayenu" (da-YE-noo). Dayenu means "it would have been enough" in Hebrew. This song tells of the blessings of God. Each blessing "would have been enough" by itself.

After the song, the bitter herbs are spread on the matzah. Haroset is mixed in to sweeten the taste. A top piece of matzah is added to make a matzah sandwich. Everyone eats. This is a symbol that even bitterness can be sweetened with hope and faith.

It is time to eat the main meal. Often the first things eaten are hard-boiled eggs flavored with salt water. Each family has favorite dishes that are part of their Passover meal. Some families have fish. Others serve lamb or chicken. Everything is delicious.

This girl is waiting for the Seder meal to begin.

Once the meal is finished, the children look for the hidden afikoman. When the afikoman is returned, the leader divides it up. Everyone at the table gets a piece. This is the last food eaten. In this way, the taste of the matzah will stay with them.

Now the door to the house is opened. The family invites in their invisible guest, Elijah. He is a symbol of hope for the Jewish people. By inviting him in, they are inviting in hope for the future.

Everyone joins in reading psalms from the Bible. More songs are sung. One of them is called "Had Gadya" (ḥad gad-YA). It is about a man who buys a young goat or kid. Sometimes there are jokes, riddles, and games.

The Seder is over. Everyone calls out, "Next year in Jerusalem, next year may all be free."

Passover week continues. In the synagogue, there are special prayers and readings. Everyone feels closer to God, closer to their history, and closer to their family.

This girl is drawing the flag of Israel.

Yom Ha-Atsma'ut

When Moses led the Jews out of Egypt, they settled in an area called Canaan (k'-NA-an). Later the land was called Israel. But after many years, Israel was invaded. The Jews were captured and scattered all over the world. They no longer had a country.

Finally in 1948 the area where Jews once lived became the country of Israel again. The fifth day of the Jewish month of Iyyar (i'-YAR) became Yom Ha-Atsma'ut, Israel's Independence Day. This is usually in April or May. In Israel there are parades, speeches, and celebrations. People sing and dance up and down the streets in every city in Israel. In the United States and Canada, Jewish people gather in synagogues and thank God for protecting their homeland.

The symbol of the celebration is the flag of Israel. The flag is white with two blue stripes. In the center is a six-sided star called the Star of David.

Israel's Independence Day is a time to remember the long history of the Jewish people. They remember their struggles. They hope that one day all people may live together in peace.

Lag B'Omer

The holiday of Lag B'Omer is celebrated on the eighteenth day of the Jewish month of Iyyar. Lag B'Omer means "thirty-three days of counting the omer." (An omer was a measure of barley.) On the second day of Passover, each farmer brought his barley, or omer, to the temple. This was something the Torah told him to do. He would say, "This is the first day of counting the omer." The counting of omer ended fifty days later on the holiday of Shavuot.

On Lag B'Omer Jews remember two very brave rabbis—Rabbi Akiba and Rabbi Shimon bar Yochai. (Rabbis are teachers. They teach people the Jewish religion and laws.) These men lived almost two thousand years ago. During this time, the Jews were under Roman rule. The Romans wanted the Jews to worship Roman gods and not teach the Jewish religion.

Rabbi Akiba was the most famous rabbi of his time. He led his students in a revolt against the Romans. The fighting went on for many days. Then a plague fell over the land. Each day students died from the plague. But then a miracle took place. On the thirty-third day of the counting of omer (Lag B'Omer), the plague stopped. This was a joyous day.

Rabbi Shimon bar Yochai refused to stop teaching the Torah and the Jewish religion. The Roman soldiers tried to kill him. He and his son ran away and hid in a cave. He continued to teach from the cave.

Every day the children came to study the Torah. They brought food for the rabbi to eat. The rabbi stayed in the cave for twelve years until finally the Roman ruler died.

Today Jewish people remember these brave men who loved their religion and the Torah. On

On Lag B'Omer some Jewish children sing songs and dance.

Lag B'Omer, many children in Hebrew schools go on picnics to remember how food was brought to the rabbi. People study the Torah and read stories about the two rabbis. In Israel children visit the grave of Rabbi Shimon bar Yochai. There they pray, sing songs, and dance.

Shavuot

Fifty days or seven weeks after Passover, Jews celebrate Shavuot. Shavuot means "weeks" in Hebrew. It occurs on the sixth day of the Jewish month of Sivan (si-VAN). This is sometime in May or June. Long ago this holiday celebrated the spring harvest. The first fruits and grains were taken to the temple. These gifts were an offering to God. It was a way to thank God for blessing them with good crops. Today people decorate their homes and synagogues with flowers and plants to get ready for Shavuot.

Many people believe that the spring harvest occurred at the same time that Moses received the Ten Commandments from God. (The Ten Commandments are laws that tell people how they should live and treat one another.) The holiday is also called the "Season of the Giving of the Law."

On Shavuot a special part of the synagogue service is the reading of the Ten Commandments. Another part is the reading from the book of Ruth. Ruth was not born Jewish. She married a Jewish man and became Jewish by choice. When her husband died, she stayed with her husband's family. The story took place at harvest time.

Flowers and plants are used to decorate homes for Shavuot.

Many boys and girls in their teens have a ceremony called "confirmation" in their synagogue on Shavuot. This comes after many years of study of Hebrew and the Jewish religion. Now they become full members of their synagogue. In some Jewish day schools, first graders receive their own prayer book and Bible for Shavuot.

After the ceremony in the synagogue, everyone goes home to have a big meal. Holiday food for Shavuot always includes lots of dairy products. Dairy products are eaten because the law is said to be like "milk and honey" to the Jewish people. Others say it is because Israel is a land "flowing with milk and honey." Cheesecake, ice cream, and blintzes are often served. (A blintz is a rolled pancake stuffed with cheese.) Children can hardly wait to eat the blintzes.

✧ ✧ ✧ ✧

These five holidays remind the Jewish people of their history. Each year they look forward to their future and the holidays to come.

Glossary

Adar—The twelfth month of the Jewish calendar. Purim is celebrated during this month.

afikoman—A piece of matzah that is hidden at the beginning of the Seder. It is eaten at the end of the meal.

Exodus—The second book of the Bible. It tells how Moses led the Jewish people from slavery in Egypt to freedom in a new land.

fast—To go without food or water for a certain period of time.

grogger—A noisemaker that a child shakes or twirls on Purim.

Haggadah—A special book read during the Seder that tells the story of the Exodus and the meaning of the food on the table.

hamantaschen—Little three-cornered cakes filled with prunes or poppy seeds and honey. They are eaten on Purim.

haroset—A mixture of chopped fruit, nuts, and wine eaten at a Seder. The mixture reminds Jews of the mortar used by their ancestors to make bricks in Egypt.

Hebrew—The language of Judaism and the Jewish people.

Iyyar—The eighth month of the Jewish calendar. Israel's Independence Day is celebrated during this month.

Lag B'Omer—A holiday that remembers the brave deeds of Rabbi Akiba and Rabbi Shimon bar Yochai when the Jews lived under Roman rule.

leaven—Any substance, like yeast, that allows bread dough to rise.

matzah—Flat bread made without yeast. It is eaten on Passover.

Megillah—The scroll that tells the story of Queen Esther. It is read in synagogues on Purim.

Nisan—The seventh month of the Jewish calendar. Passover is celebrated during this month.

Passover (Pesach)—This holiday remembers the time when Moses led the Jews from Egypt and slavery.

plague—A disease or anything that causes great misfortune.

prophet—A special person who tells others messages from God.

Purim—This holiday remembers when Queen Esther saved the Jews from a wicked man named Haman.

Sabbath—The holiest day of the week for Jews; it begins before sundown on Fridays and ends after sunset on Saturdays.

Seder—A special meal that is eaten on the first night of Passover and follows a certain order.

Shavuot—A harvest holiday that also celebrates God giving Moses the Ten Commandments.

Sivan—The ninth month of the Jewish calendar.

synagogue—A building where Jewish people come together to pray to God, learn about their religion, and be with other Jews.

Torah—A long parchment scroll that contains the first five books of the Bible.

Yom Ha-Atsma'ut—Israel's Independence Day.

Index

A Adar, 11, 12, 14
afikoman, 28, 30, 33

C Canaan, 35

E Egypt, 6, 16, 17, 20, 22, 27, 30, 35
Elijah, 27, 33
Exodus, 20, 22

G groggers, 14, 15

H Haggadah, 29, 30
hamantaschen, 14
haroset, 25, 26, 31
Hebrew, 9, 29, 31, 40, 41, 43

I Israel, 7, 34, 35, 36, 40, 43
Iyyar, 35, 37

J Jerusalem, 26, 33
Judaism, 9

L Lag B'Omer, 5, 7, 37, 38, 39, 40

M matzah, 21, 22, 25, 26, 27, 28, 31
Megillah, 14
Moses, 6, 7, 16, 17, 18, 19, 22, 30, 35, 41

N Nisan, 17

P Passover, 5, 6, 17, 18, 21, 22, 23, 24, 31, 33, 37, 41
Purim, 4, 5, 6, 11, 12, 14, 15

R Red Sea, 19, 27

S Sabbath, 9, 27
Seder, 23, 24, 25, 26, 28, 29, 32, 33
Shavuot, 5, 7, 37, 41, 42, 43
Sivan, 41
synagogue, 4, 9, 14, 33, 36, 41, 43

T Ten Commandments, 7, 41, 42
Torah, 8, 9, 37, 38, 40

Y Yom Ha-Atsma'ut, 5, 7, 35